Building Websites for Beginners

Introduction to WordPress, Joomla, Wix and Drupal

Nate Jenner

Table of Contents

Disclaimer

While all attempts have been made to verify the information provided in this book, the author does assume any responsibility for errors, omissions, or contrary interpretations of the subject matter contained within. The information provided in this book is for educational and entertainment purposes only. The reader is responsible for his or her own actions and the author does not accept any responsibilities for any liabilities or damages, real or perceived, resulting from the use of this information.

The trademarks that are used are without any consent, and the publication of the trademark is without permission or backing by the trademark owner. All trademarks and brands within this book are for clarifying purposes only and are the owned by the owners themselves, not affiliated with this document.

Introduction

The need for websites is on the rise. Individuals are now developing websites where you can be able to access information about them. Others are also in need of blogs through which you can get an opportunity to engage them and others in a discussion. Businesses, institutions and companies are all in need of websites. Traditionally, the development of a website involved writing of thousands of lines of programming code. However, this has changed recently. You can design and develop a complete website without having to write a single line of code. Yes, an international and completely looking website. This is possible by use of a number of tools most of which are available for free use. You only have to download them then begin building your website. Others provide you with an online platform where you can develop your website. This book discusses such tools and platforms and helps you know the steps you should go through in order to develop a website with them. Enjoy!

Chapter 1- Getting Started with Website Development

Websites have become so popular such that each and every business is running a website. Websites are a common way of communication between a business and its clients. Websites can be basic or complex. You can choose to build a website simply on which people will be able to get information related to your business, institution or company. This is the most basic type of website, and they are so popular in the world today. You can also build a complex website with complex features such as paying for goods and services, video calls etc. The e-commerce websites such as Amazon.com are a good example of such websites. Users are allowed to make purchases for various types of goods and services using various payment methods.

There are various ways for one to develop a website. One can use pure programming languages to develop a website. Examples of such programming languages are PHP and Python. However, development of a website through pure programming can be a complex task, and at the same time consuming. Due to this, systems have been developed for web developers to have an easy way of developing websites. With these systems, you don't have to do any form of coding.

Good examples of such systems are the content management systems like Joomla, WordPress and Drupal. With such, you can create a website within a short period of time even without knowledge about any programming language. These systems are taking over web development as most people are now preferring them rather than coding a website from scratch. The systems come with various themes that you can use to enhance the look and feel of your website. There are also plugins that can be used to add various functionalities to your website. Basically, the development of websites using such systems simply involves installations.

Chapter 2- Web Development with WordPress

What is WordPress?

WordPress is a content management system (CMS) that can be used for development of blogs and websites. It is popularly used for development of blogs. It can be said to be the easiest to use of all the available CMSs. There are numerous themes and plugins that can be used for web development with WordPress. The themes are used to enhance the user interface of the website while the plugins come with additional features that are not available in the WordPress itself. Some themes and plugins are available for a free use, while others are commercial. For some, you are only required to pay the purchasing fee while for others; one is required to pay a monthly or yearly subscription fee.

Let us discuss how to develop a website with WordPress in a step-by-step manner:

Setup

Most users prefer to use a self-hosted WordPress.org website. This provides you with various designs and add-ons that you can use to develop your own website.

You can download and use WordPress for free. You are only required to organizer for your domain name as well as hosting. The domain name is the address of your website on the internet. You can simply buy it on Godaddy.com

You can create an account on Bluehost.com and you will find it easy to install WordPress. However, you can also develop a website on the localhost, that is, your computer, in which the computer will act as the server. However, ensure your computer has the following:

1. Database. Use MySQL 5.0 +

2. Web Server. Use WAMP (Windows), LAMP (Linux), XAMP (Multi-platform), MAMP (Macintosh)

3. Operating System. WordPress is Cross-platform.

4. Browser. Use either IE (Internet Explorer 8+), Google chrome, Firefox, Safari or Opera

5. PHP 5.2+

Next, download WordPress from:
https://wordpress.org/download/.

You only have to click the "Download WordPress ..." button located to the right of the screen.

WordPress requires a MySQL database in your system. Login to your MySQL database as the root user then create an empty database that will be used by WordPress. You create an empty database and WordPress will create the necessary tables automatically in that database. During the installation, WordPress will ask you to specify the name of the database.

Now that you have created the database, it is time for you to setup the WordPress. Extract the WordPress package (setup) that you have downloaded then transfer it to web server or the localhost. If you are transferring it to the localhost and you are using WampServer, this is normally the "www" folder.

Next, open your browser then navigate to the path in which you have stored the WordPress. In my case, I have placed the WordPress in the www folder of WampServer installation. If I navigate to that directory on the browser, I am able to see it under the "Your Projects" tab:

Just click it. You will be asked to choose the language you need to use then click "Continue". In the next step, information about the database requirements will be shown. Read through then click ""Let's go".

In the next screen, enter information the MySQL database. The "Database Name" is the name of the MySQL database that you have created for the WordPress site. The "Username" is the name you use to log into the MySQL database. The Password is the password that you have created for MySQL database. The "Database Host" is the name of the host or computer, which takes a default value of "localhost". The "Table Prefix" value will be used as the prefix when giving names to the database tables.

Once you have completed filling all the information, click the "Submit" button. WordPress will check whether you have provided correct database information and you will get a confirmations screen. Click the button written "Run the install".

Next, you should provide the administrative information. The site title is the name of the website that you are developing. Also, enter a username and a password that you will be using to log into the administrative panel of the website. Also, ensure that you add your email address. Once you have filled all the information that is required, click the "Install WordPress" button.

After a successful installation of WordPress, you will see a success screen. Click the "Log In" button then use the username and password that you created to login. After a successful login, you will be taken to the WordPress dashboard.

Selecting a Theme

The purpose of a WordPress theme is to control the visual appearance of your website. They are professionally-designed templates that you can install to change the appearance of your website. By default, every WordPress website has a basic theme. However, this may not be appealing to the users, so you have to change it. There are thousands of WordPress themes available for both fee and commercial basis.

The admin dashboard allows you to change the theme for your WordPress site. Click "Appearance" then choose "Themes". To add a new one, click the "Add New" button.

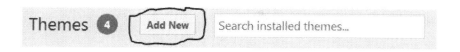

In the next page, you will have the option of searching for the available themes on WordPress.org. Once the theme you need to use is found, click the "Install" button and it will be installed.

If you need to customize the theme that you have installed, you only have to click the "Customize" link located below the Appearance menu. However, you will only learn how to customize it well once you have added content to your website.

Adding Website Content

There are two types of content in WordPress, pages and posts. Pages are meant to be static, whereas posts are part of the blog appearing in reverse-chronological order. In WordPress, the blog posts are added to the front page of the website. However, it is possible for you to change this. You can begin by adding some pages to your website.

If you don't enough content for these, note that you can edit it later.

In the WordPress admin area, click on "Pages", then choose "Add New". You must enter a title for the page, then its content below that:

Note that you can add any type of content to the page including audio, video, pictures etc. Once you are done with adding content for the page, you will be able to create the "Publish" button in order to make the page live on the website.

To add extra pages to the website, you will have to repeat the same steps and you will be able to create pages for Home, About us, Contact us etc.

To add blog posts to the website, click on "Posts" then choose "Add New". You will get a screen that is similar to that of creating new pages.

Once you are done with adding content for the post, just click the "Publish" button located on the right side and it will appear live on your website.

Creating a Static Front Page

Now that your website has come content, you can customize it so that it can appear well on the website. On the WordPress admin area, click "Settings" then "Reading". Under the option for "Front page displays", click the static front page then choose "Pages" you had created for the home and blogs. Save the changes by clicking on "Save Changes" button located at the bottom in order to save the changes.

The page you have chosen will then be used as the front page for your website as well as the blog pages.

Changing Title and Tagline

During the installation of WordPress, you are allowed to create a title for your site. WordPress will automatically add a tagline to the site title. The default text for the tagline is "Just another WordPress site". However, it is possible for you to change the title and tagline for your site anytime you want by clicking "Settings" then choosing "General". Note that you can leave the tagline field blank if you wish.

Note that the site title is the name for your website. The tagline helps you describe your website.

Comment Settings

WordPress provides default comment system that allows users to write comments about your posts. It is a good of enhancing user engagement, but spammers have misused it. Only what you need to do is enable comment moderation on the website.

Click "Settings" then "Discussion" then scroll down to "Before a comment appears" section. Check the box for "Comments must be manually approved:

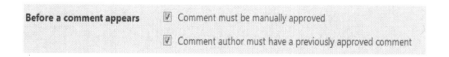

Once done, click the "Save Changes" button so that the changes can be saved and applied.

Creating Navigation Menus

With navigation menus, users are able to browse different pages on your website. WordPress provides us with a very powerful navigation system which your theme must adhere to in order to display the menus. Let us create a navigation menu for the website.

Click "Appearance" then choose "Menus". Provide a name to the navigation menu then click the create menu button. WordPress will then create the navigation menu.

In the next step, you are expected to select the pages that you need to add to the navigation menu. Once done, click the add to menu button. The pages you have selected will then fill the empty area of the navigation menu. It is possible for you to move them up and rearrange how they are positioned on the menu.

You should now select the display location. Your WordPress theme defines these locations. In most themes, the menu appears on the top of the website. Once done, click the Save button to save the changes.

Installing Plugins

The plugins are similar to the apps for your website. They allow you to add extra features to your WordPress website. Through WordPress plugins, you are able to add features such as the contact form, galleries and others to your website. Currently, there are over 49,000 plugins available for use in WordPress. There are also third-party plugins that are being sold by developers.

Plugins are easy for you to use as you only have to install then activate it. There are various ways for you to install plugins for your website.

If you need to install a particular plugin to your website, begin by downloading it to your computer. Next, on the administration panel of WordPress, navigate to the left navigation bar then click Plugins. Choose "Add New". Browse to where you have stored the plugin in your computer then select it. Next, click "Install Now" and you will have the plugin installed. You can also find the plugin that you want by choosing from the Featured, Popular, Recommended and Favorites sections, or even by typing the name of the plugin in the search field in order to search for it.

At this point, you should be able to create your own website with WordPress.

Chapter 3- Web Development with Wix

The creation of a website with Wix is a free and straightforward process. However, if you are unfamiliar with the platform, you may find it challenging to do so. It provides a number of options to those in need of creating a website, and this can leave them confused.

Wix is a website that you can access Wix.com. Everything on Wix is provided for free, but you must for you to get a custom domain and unlimited bandwidth.

Signing Up for an Account

For you to get started with Wix, you are required to sign up for an account in the same way you could sign up for any online service. Wix allows you to sign with your Facebook or Google account, but you can as well use your email address and create a password in order to sign in.

Choose the Website Type

You are expected to choose a type for the website in order to start. First, open wix.com on your browser then click the "Create Your Website" button.

Welcome to Wix

Let's get your website online today!

You will then be provided with a number of options from which you can choose one.

What kind of website do you want to create?

Business >	Designer >	Blog >
Online Store >	Restaurants & Food >	Beauty & Wellness >
Photography >	Accommodation >	Portfolio & CV >
Music >	Events >	Other >

Just choose the kind of website you need to create from the available options. Remember that the option that you choose will determine the options as well as the templates that you will be provided with later. This is why you should make sure that you choose the best one based on your business and the kind of features that you need your website to have.

Select a Template

Wix provides you with an easy way of creating a website in which you will only be required to provide the details of your website and it will be created for you. However, the end product may not be what you like, hence it will be good for you to use the Wix Editor and create the website the way you want. This is what we are going to do.

Now that you have chosen the kind of website that you need to create, it is time for you to choose a template for the website. Instead of using the Wix ADI, we will be using the Wix Editor. Click the "Choose a Template" button:

Create Your Website with the Wix Editor

Start with a template and make it your own, with easy drag and drop & 1000s of design features.

Choose a Template

You will be provided with various templates, so you must choose the template that you need to use. You will notice that these templates will be categorized into various groups including consultants, service providers or marketers etc. You can click on each category and choose the template that you need, or even search for what you are looking for. You will also notice most of the available websites can be used for free.

To preview how your website will look when using a particular template, point at the template then click "View". You can click the "Edit this site" button to edit the look of the website. This is the only way you can get the website that you need.

Click Edit and create your own amazing website   Read More   Edit this site

The Wix Editor will then be started.

Creating Pages

In the next page where you have the Wix editor, you will be able to add new pages to the site. You only have to click the "Menus & Pages" option on the left side of the screen.

All the available pages for the website will be shown. To add a new page, click the "Add Page" button on the bottom:

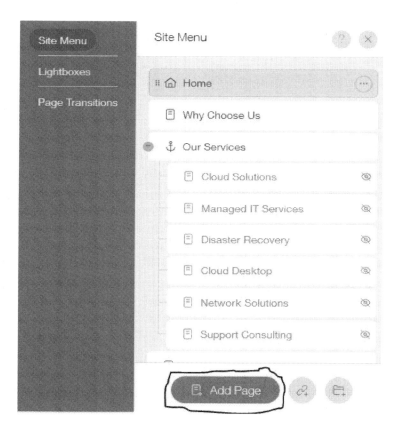

The new page window will pop up where you should provide a name for the page. Anytime that you want to delete a page, you only have to click the icon with three ... on the right and choose the "Delete" option as shown below:

After clicking the Delete option, you will be asked to confirm the deletion and the page will be deleted. Note that the pages you find there will be the default ones for the theme you chose. This is why you should delete all of them and create your own, the ones that fit what your business offers.

Changing the Background

It is possible for you to change the background appearance of your wix website. On the wix editor, move the mouse cursor to the left of the window and click the "Background" icon. The following window will pop up from the side:

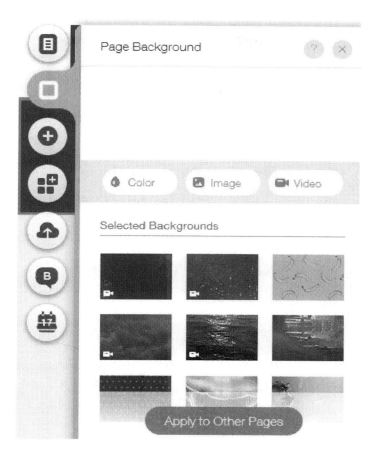

From the above window, you are able to set a background color, image or even video. To change the background color, click on "color", then select a color that you need from the available ones. Once you have clicked the correct one, close the color picker. Note that the color you have chosen will only be applied to the current page. For you to apply it to the other pages, just click the button written "Apply to Other Pages".

To change the background image, click on "Images" option and a new window will pop up. For you to add new images, click the "Upload Images" button on the top right corner of the screen.

Once you have chosen the image to apply to the background, click the "Change Background" button on the bottom right of the window. The background of the site will then change to use that site.

Wix also provides you with various ways of getting images to use at the background of the site. Other than uploading images from your computer, you can choose images from social media platforms such as Facebook, Instagram etc. Wix also provides you with images which you can use for free. The Shutterstock window has professionally created images that you can purchase and use on your website.

Adding Different Elements

The template only acts as the starting point for your website. It is possible for you to add various other elements to the pages in a bid to make the website more appealing. There are a number of potential elements that you can add to your page, and you can find them by clicking the "Add" option/icon on the left side of the window:

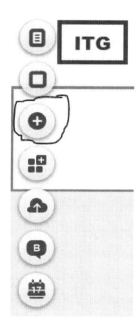

All the elements that you can add to your page will be shown on the new window on the left side. Some of the elements that you can add include text boxes, images, slideshows, buttons, menus, videos or shapes. Click on any of them and you will be provided with various options showing the styles you can use to add them to your page. You will then have the option of adding the elements to the site.

Once you have added a particular element to a page, you should not forget to do the same for the other pages.

Adding a Blog

It is possible for you to choose the pages to be included in the website. One of such pages that you can add is the blog if you had not added it to the main web page. You can use the tools from the sidebar to add your blog to the website.

You only have to click the icon labeled B and written "My Blog":

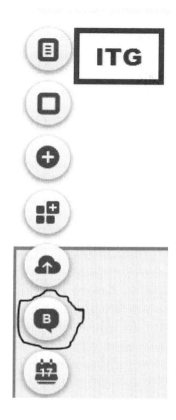

A new window will pop up, on which you only have to click the "Add Now" button. You will be taken to the window for Blog Manager. If you need to create a new blog post, click the button for "Add a New Blog Post". On the left, click the option for "Blog Pages". You will see the name that will appear on the website so that users click it to access the blog. To change or rename this, just click the icon with ... to the right then choose "Rename" and you will be allowed to change its name.

The management of the blog can be done by clicking the "Add Blog Elements" option on the left side of the window. Some of the elements that you can add to your blog include:

- Disqus comments
- Facebook comments
- Custom feed
- RSS
- Categories
- And others

Other than the above elements, you can also add some wix apps that will add power to the blog. You will also find that Wix has populated the blog with some posts, making it easy for you to just edit and publish them instead of beginning from scratch.

Anytime that you want to see how your website looks like, just click the "preview" option on the top right of the screen.

To publish the website, you must click the "Publish" button next to the "Preview" button. Anytime you are in the preview mode, you can always go back to the Wix editor by clicking the button on the top right corner of the screen.

Before publishing the website, preview it first to ensure that you have set everything in the way you want it to be.

Chapter 4- Web Development with Joomla

Joomla is one of the popular content management systems that have revolutionized the web development industry. Some of the world renowned brands have used Joomla to build their websites. Examples of these include Harvard University, MTV, Heathrow Airport, Peugeot, High Court of Australia, UK Ministry of Defense, General Electric, and eBay. The reason behind this is that Joomla is very powerful.

Installing Joomla

You can buy a domain and do web development online. Also, it is possible for you to install Joomla on your local machine and use the computer as the server. To make it easy for your understanding, installation of Joomla on a localhost can do in the same way we did for WordPress. You only to download Joomla have MySQL and create a Joomla database within MySQL. You then open the Joomla on the browser and you will be taken through the installation steps. Lastly, you will be at the administrator panel, the panel. Whenever you need to access the administrator area, you should type */administrator* after the URL name.

Template Installation

In Joomla, we use a template rather than a theme as it is the case with WordPress. Templates are extensions, so they are installed from the *Extensions* part of the system.

Click Extensions; choose "Extension Manager", then browser for the extension file. Next, click "Upload & Install".

Joomla will also provide you with the options given below for installing extensions:

1. Install from web- this involves installing the extension from the Joomla Extension Directory (JED).

2. Install from directory- here, the user is allowed to specify the path to the directory with the extension.

3. Install from URL- the user is allowed to enter the URL to the extension.

Note that there are various sites online from which you can download templates. Some of the templates are available for free while others are on sale.

Once the template has been installed, you need to activate it. To do this, go to Extensions, and then choose "Template Manager". On the screen for template manager, find the template then click the star on the right in order to set it as the default. The template will be activated on the website, but it will be good for you to visit the website in order to confirm this.

Adding Website Content

In Joomla, the content is identified by the word Article. The articles are grouped into categories then organized in the menu.

Ti creates a new article; click the "Add New Article" option on the left of the control panel. Give the article a name as well as other content such as images etc. To add an image to the article, you only have to click the "Image" button located on the bottom of the editor.

All the articles for the website will be kept in the "Article Manager". This is where you can view all the articles that you have for the website.

You can also make a particular article to be featured so that it may be shown on the front page of the website. To do this, you only have to click the star located next to the article.

Creating Menu

If an article has not been added to a menu, it will not appear on the website. It is less likely that one will need to add their article to the default menu of the website. In most cases, you will need to create your own menu. To do this, go to "Menu Manager" then choose "Add New Menu". You can then create a title, type and description for the menu. Once done, save then close the screen by clicking "Save & Close".

After that, you should begin adding the menu items. To do this, click Menus, choose "New Menu" then click "Add New Menu Items".

You will be required to choose a type for the menu item. You will be provided with the following options:

Menu Item Type

Articles

Configuration Manager

Contacts

News Feeds

Search

Smart Search

System Links

Tags

Choose "Articles" as the menu item type. You will get a new list, but choose single article. You can then select the article that you need to display on the menu.

However, for the menu to be displayed on the website, it must be assigned a module position, so you are yet to complete.

Adding a Module

Go to Extensions, click "Module Manager" then click New. A pop up will appear. Select the "Menu" option and you will be taken to module configuration page. Give the module a title then choose the menu. You can then go to positions then choose a position for the menu module for your drop down list.

After that, you will be able to see the menu on the website. Feel free to create similar pages by following the same steps.

Creating a Contact Us Page

The "Contact Us" form is a very important part of a business. It provides customers with a way of getting in touch with you. It is also a way of creating consumer trust on a brand. Joomla comes with a contact form builder. This helps you to easily come up with a way of sending you messages.

To create the form, click on Components at the top navigation bar then choose "Contacts".

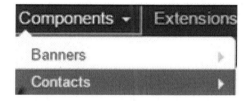

In the next page, click the "New" button located on the top left of the screen.

Add the contact person that you need to use for the form. The contact should also be given a name as well as an email address.

The messages send by the clients will be directed to the email address that you provide. After filling all the necessary information, click "Save & Close".

Now that you have created the form, you should add it to the main menu. This is the way to make it accessible by customers.

Follow the steps discussed previously to add a new menu item. Click the option for "Contacts" then choose "Single Contact".

Give this menu item the name "Contact Us". Click on "Select" button which is located next to Select Contact then select the account that you have made above.

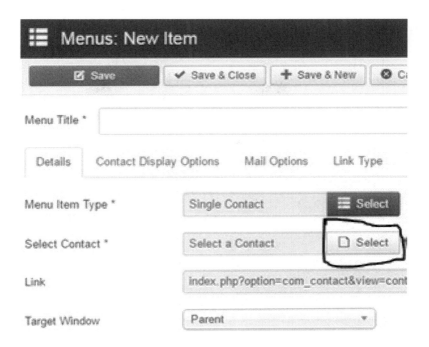

Once you have selected the account, just save and close the form and it will be added to main menu.

Chapter 5- Web Development with Drupal

Drupal is one of the powerful website building platforms available on the internet today. With Drupal, you can create a website that is fast, amazing and efficient. However, it might be a bit confusing for you to get started with developing websites with Drupal; especially of you are beginners.

Begin beginning to build the website, first make sure that you have a solid domain name. After getting the domain name, identify and get a web hosting service. Bluehost is the best company in web hosting, so you can choose them.

Downloading and Installing Drupal

This is a very easy process. It can be done in the same way that you did with WordPress and Joomla. The process even becomes simpler if you are using a web hosting service provider such as Bluehost as the installation can be done in simply a single click of a button.

Once the installation is completed, you should begin building your website. Your site will be given the title "My Site' as the default one. This is so boring; hence you need to choose a site for your website.

If you have a business name that you need to develop the website for, then you can use that name as the name for the website.

If you need to change the name of the site, click "Configuration", choose "Site Information". In the field for "Site Name", type the name of the site. If you have a slogan, just enter it into the Slogan field. This can also be the tagline, just some text that describes what your site is about.

SITE DETAILS

Site name *

Slogan

How this is used depends on your site's theme.

E-mail address *

The *From* address in automated e-mails sent during registration and new password requests, and prevent this e-mail being flagged as spam.)

Ensure that the email address that you entered during installation is shown in the "Email" field. Save the changes you make to the site then go back to the home page of the site. You may have to refresh the page in order to see whether the changes have taken effect or not.

Selecting a Theme

The original Drupal theme may not look good, so you may have to change it. To see any additional themes, follow the steps given below:

1. Open the "Appearance" menu.

2. Click on "Install New Theme".

3. Click on "Themes" and you will be taken to a page several themes.

Since you will be presented with numerous themes, you may find it hard to select the best theme for your site. However, ensure that you choose a theme that is responsive, meaning that your site will appear well on all devices despite their screen sizes. The theme should also be easy to customize, meaning that it may require you to do only a less coding. However, this will be determined by the kind of customization that you need on your site. The theme should also be visually attractive in order to attract people to your site. If you don't know how to code, or if you don't like it, note that there are plenty of themes that don't require you to do any kind of coding. Note that there are also themes that are the best for Drupal beginners.

Creating a New Page

You may be in need of creating the Home, About Us or any other kind of page. You may add content to your pages so that you may describe who you are and the services offered by your business. To setup the page, follow the steps given below:

1. Navigate through "Content" -> "Add Content" -> "Basic Page".

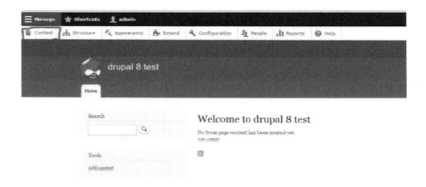

2. In the Title field, type a name for the page, maybe Home, About us, then adds information to the page in the "Body" section.

3. Since we need the page to be shown in the menu, check the box written "Provide A Menu Link" under the Menu Settings. You can then save the changes and you will be able to see the page on the main menu.

4. You may be in need of changing the order of the items. In such a case, navigate through Structure -> Menus -> Main Menu. To shift the items, you only have to grab the small crosses using your mouse then drag then up and down.

You can use the same approach discussed above in order to create other pages for the website.

Adding Contributed Modules

Drupal has a very loyal and supportive community. This community is much responsible in contributing very good modules to the Drupal community. The following steps will help you add a module to your Drupal website:

1. Begin by downloading the tar or zip file to your system.

2. If you are developing your website online like on a web hosting service provider like Bluehost, upload this module to the sites/all/modules" directory where you have installed the Drupal. The upload can be done using a FTP client such as FileZilla. If you are developing the site locally, you don't need to use the FTP client.

3. Unzip the files then enable them from the Admin/Modules section of the website.

Just like themes, there are a number of modules that you can choose. However, there are a number of modules that you should add to your Drupal installation. Let us discuss some of these modules:

Admin Menu Module

When using the default toolbar, a lot of time is wasted when loaded numerous pages in order to get a single admin area. However, you can use the Admin Menu Module to avoid this. This menu provides you with drop-down menus for the whole admin area.

You only have to turn off the "Toolbar" that you are using then activate the Admin Menu Module.

CKEditor Module

In Drupal, the default WYSIWYG (What You See Is What You Get) text editor is not provided. This text editor provides a visual HTML text area editor which is similar to the common word processors. The text is made to be visually more appealing and easy to format.

The following steps will help you make the module work:

1. Install Drupal Module, and then download the standalone CKEditor by visiting the download section of CKEditor.com.

2. You can then unpack the files in the sites /all /modules /ckeditor/ckeditor directory of the Drupal website.

IMCE Editor

It is always good for you to add images to your post to enhance its visual appearance. The IMCE editor helps you in adding images to your posts. The following steps will help you have a working IMCE editor:

1. Install then enable IMCE.

2. Navigate through Configuration –> Content Authoring –> CKEditor –> Profiles –> Advanced –> Edit –> File Browser Settings.

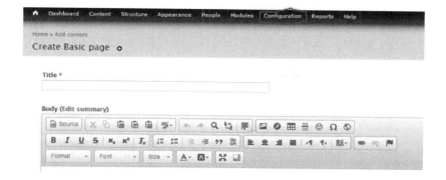

3. Choose IMCE from the link dialog window drop down as well as from image dialog and flash dialog windows.

4. Finally, save the settings.

Token Module

Tokens are sections of text added via a placeholder system. These are good for your website when you need to relay important information to the site viewers.

Pathauto Module

Drupal comes with a built-in path module that helps you create good URLs by hand. This can be tiresome to do by hand for every single post; hence the Pathauto module relieves you from this.

It is possible for you to place custom replacement patterns as well as user account page paths so that the URLs may match your SEO and usability standards. However, note that for Pathauto to work, it requires the Token module.

Views Module

With views in Drupal, you can display your content in a variety of forms from lists to slideshows. This is a good way of making your audience stay interested in your site. The views module can be a bit complicated to work with compared to the other modules, but once you know how it works, you will appreciate how important and powerful it is. In Drupal 7, you are required to install the Chaos Tools Suite module so that the Views module can work.

Chaos Tools Suite Module

The Tools or the Chaos Tools Suite is required for the Views module to work. However, this is not the only use of this module. The module provides Drupal developers with very useful features on its own. You can use this module to create your own modules, dialog boxes, forms, pluggable content types, sanitize CSS and others.

Quicktab Module

You may need to have tabbed boxes on your website that show the most recent and popular content. Quicktabs are good for creating tabbed views, blocks and nodes quickly and easily without having to write any custom JavaScript.

You should install then enable the module, and then you will find Quicktabs selection below Structure menu.

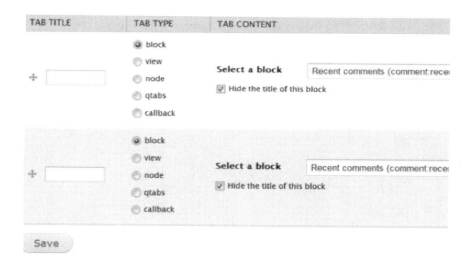

Blocks

Now that you have all the essential modules, you may be in need of having a sidebar of Blocks with different features.

The blocks are boxes of content like "User Login", "Who's Online" and they can be displayed on the header, footer, sidebar or the other regions on the page.

After creating a block, it is possible for you to adjust its appearance, size, shape and position and the pages of the website on which it should appear. You may want to add block content for "Recent Content". The following steps can help you add this:

1. Begin by navigating to Structure Blocks. You will be able to see the disabled blocks.

2. Find the block for "Recent Content" then look across to Region column:

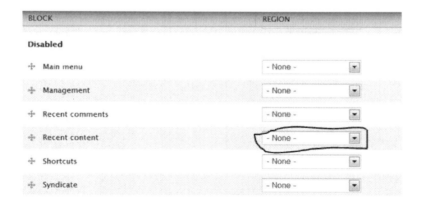

3. You can choose the region in which you need the content to be displayed. You will be

provided by several regions that you can choose depending on the theme that you are using.

4. Save the page for blocks then go back to the front page.

5. For you to add content, click on "Add New Content", click Article then give it a title. Fill in the pertinent tags then add some text to the body part.

6. Save the article then move back to the main site. You will be able to see that the article appears as well as the block with Recent Content.

Adding a Blog

Blogs are becoming an essential to every website today and they provide the website owner with a way of sharing news with their audience. It will be good for you to add a blog to your Drupal website.

Add Content Type

For you to add some blog to your Drupal website, you should first open the Structure tab then click "Content types" menu.

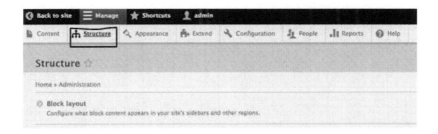

Next, click the button for "Add content type" and this will open the page for content creation. After selecting a name for the content type, click the button for "Save and change fields".

Adding Comment Field

Now that the content type is ready, you can navigate to Structure -> Content types again. The newly created content type should be available in the list.

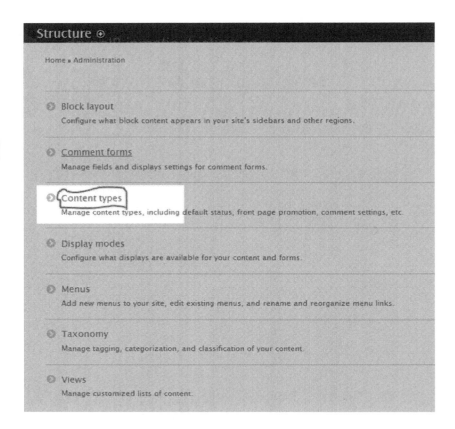

From the drop-down menu for "Manage fields" for "Blog" content type, choose "Add field".

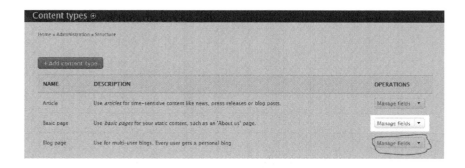

From the drop-down for "Re-use an existing field", select "Comments: comment". If you need, you can edit the label then hit "Save and continue" when done. In Drupal 8, the default setting is that non-registered users are not allowed to post their comments. If you need to allow users who are not yet registered to be able to leave their comments, it will be good for you to configure the blog accordingly.

Click the tab for "People" then choose "Permissions" section in order to review the options that are available. If you also need to allow the anonymous users to leave their comments, just check the box for "Post comments" located below "Anonymous user". If you want to be able to verify comments from anonymous users before they can appear on the blog, leave the option for "Skip comment approval" unticked. Once you are done with changing the settings, just click the "Save settings" button to save them.

Creating the Blog Page

It is now time for you to create a new blog page. This can be done by navigating through Content -> Add content. Ensure that you choose the Blog content type.

Once you have adjusted the Title, URL alias as well as other settings, just click the "Save" button. Your blog will then be ready.

Approving Comments

After an anonymous has posted their comment on your blog post, they will be notified that the comment is awaiting approval. To see all the unapproved comments, you can navigate through Content menu > Comments tab > Unapproved comments.

Click the "Action" drop-down and choose what you want to do with the comment. You can delete or publish the comment. After that, click the button for "Apply to selected items".

You will then get an awesome blog in Drupal.

Adding Contact Us Page

A contact page is a good way of getting feedback from users. It is easy for you to create one in Drupal. First, open the Extend page then enable the Contact module. This module comes pre-installed with Drupal and even enabled in some Drupal versions. Your work is just to check whether it is enabled or not.

Next, navigate through Structure -> Contact forms. You will notice that you are provided with a default contact form. However, it is possible for you to edit it for your convenience.

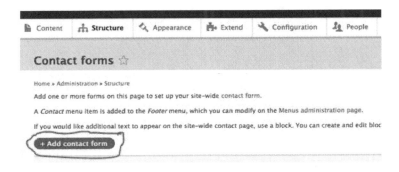

Adding Link to the Menu

Our goal is now to add this form to the menu. Navigate through Structure > Menus > Main navigation then click the arrow located next to "Edit menu" button. You will see the "Add link" button, so just click it.

Granting Permissions

Now that you have created the form and added it to the menu, you need to allow users to be able to use the form. Open the "Extend" page then click the "Permissions" link located next to "Contact" module.

You will find the Contact section, then place a checkbox in the column for "ANONYMOUS USER" for "Use the site-wide contact form" then click the "Save permissions" button located at the bottom of the page.

After that, go back to the website and see how your brand new contact form appears.

Adding Social Media Links

Some versions of Drupal come installed with social media module that allows you to social media icons with links to your Drupal website.

This can be done through the theme settings. In the latest versions such as Drupal 8, this module is not pre-installed, so you must install manually to your site in order to be able to add the social media icons to your website.

Let us begin by downloading and installing the Social Media Links Block and Field module. To install the module, go to the "Extend" menu then click on "Install new module" button.

Click the "Choose file" then browse to the directory you have kept the downloaded file. Click the "Install" button. Once the module is installed, you should enable it by going to the EXTEND section then looking for the OTHER section.

You will be able to see Social Media Links Block and Social Media Links field. Ensure that you have ticked both of these then clicks the "Install" button.

Once you have installed and enabled the module successfully, navigate through Structure > Block layout then select where you need to add the block.

If you need to add it to the footer section of the website, click the "Place block" button located next to Footer.

You will see a pop up with the available social buttons and it appears where you need to add the related URLs. Once you have added the URLs that you desire, click the "Save Block" button located at the bottom of the page.

After that, you will get the social media icons on your website. People will be able to click them and be directed to your social media accounts.

Adding Facebook Embedded Comments

It is easy for you to add the various social media boxes. You only have to get code from the social media platform that you need to link. We will be adding the Facebook embedded comments and these steps can also be used for adding Facebook like button, the Twitter Feed and different widgets.

Begin by navigating through Structure > Block layout > Custom block then click the button for "Add custom block".

You can add a description for the block. You can then paste the code you have obtained from Facebook, Twitter or the other social media networks. Also, ensure you are in plain text mode and the editor has been set to FULL HTML. Once done, click on "Save" button then add a custom block to the footer top bar or any other block of the website.

That is how you can get a website with Drupal. However, it may take some time for you to harness and appreciate the power of Drupal. The learning process normally takes some time, and the best way for you to learn how to do web development with Drupal is by playing around with it.

Conclusion

This marks the end of this book. For you to develop a website, it is not a must for you to have knowledge about computer programming. There are several tools and platforms that can help you create a website without writing a single line of code. Most of these tools and platforms are available for a free use. Most of these fall under the category of content management systems. With these, you are only required to download a theme or a template with good visual design to enhance the look and feel of your website. The rest of the web content becomes easy to install once the theme/template is installed on the website. The rest of the website functionalities can be added via plugins and modules. Themes, templates, plugins and modules ay are available for a free use or they may be commercial. The commercial ones may require you to make a one-time purchase, while for others; you may be required to pay for subscription every month or year.

The most popular tools that can be used for web development without coding include WordPress, Joomla, Wix and Drupal. WordPress is the simplest of all, followed by Joomla, then Wix and lastly Drupal. However, none of them is hard to use. You only have to play around with them and you will get used to how they work.

Manufactured by Amazon.ca
Bolton, ON

27813504R00037